Original title:
The Fig's Legacy

Copyright © 2025 Creative Arts Management OÜ
All rights reserved.

Author: Penelope Hawthorne
ISBN HARDBACK: 978-1-80586-247-5
ISBN PAPERBACK: 978-1-80586-719-7

Echoes of Ancient Harvests

In gardens where laughter sings,
The fruit wore tiny crowns of bling.
A squirrel held a nutty feast,
While birds cheered like a lively beast.

Farmers danced in their old shoes,
Chasing dreams and playful blues.
With every pluck, a giggle flew,
As the figs turned ripe, the fun just grew.

Beneath the Gnarled Tree

Beneath the tree so wise and old,
Stories of mischief still unfold.
A raccoon in search of snacks galore,
Stole the picnic while folks snore.

The figs whispered tales of fools,
As children played their silly rules.
With sticky hands and joyful shrieks,
They climbed the branches for cheeky peaks.

Secrets of the Orchard

In orchards lush with shade and cheer,
The fruits conspired, oh so near.
A bee in shades of polka-dots,
Buzzed by with plans on spicy plots.

With each pluck, a giggle stirred,
As if the figs had overheard.
Neighbors shared their baking dreams,
While pies erupted with sweet cream streams.

A Tapestry of Ripeness

A patchwork quilt of colors bright,
In sunlit fields, what a sight!
Ants in conga lines paraded round,
While laughter echoed through the ground.

As flavors danced in summer's breeze,
The figs were scheming, if you please.
With every bite, a smile grew wide,
In this merry world, none could hide.

Underneath the Vibrant Canopy

Underneath the vibrant leaves,
Squirrels plot their daring heists;
They snatch the fruits from greedy bees,
And dance like they're in wild feasts.

A bird in blue, with flair so grand,
Flies in to show off his bright style;
While laughter spreads across the land,
As branches sway, and giggles pile.

In every twist, a secret stash,
Of nuts and figs, they hide with glee;
The woodland critters share a laugh,
As they snack under the old fig tree.

Who knew such fun could come to be,
From little fruits up in the sky?
A feast of joy, what wild spree,
Beneath the branches, laughing high!

Nature's Timeless Gift

In gardens where the laughter rings,
A fig tree stands, so proud and bright,
It spills its bounty, gives us flings,
With fruity laughter, pure delight.

The ants march in a grand parade,
Their tiny heads held high with pride;
They carry snacks, a feast well paid,
While all the bugs just smile wide.

A gopher plots a sneaky dive,
To swipe a fig without a care;
He twirls and rolls, what joy, alive!
As laughter fills the sunny air.

So here's to nature's bumpy ride,
Where fruits unite and friends collide;
With funny antics, joy, and cheer,
Each harvest day, we draw near!

Ripening Under the Sun

A fruit with a funny face,
Growing in its sunny space.
Swaying gently in the breeze,
Silly thoughts among the leaves.

Little critters having fun,
Dancing 'round as day is done.
They giggle, laugh, and then they sway,
As figs just ripen day by day.

Ancestral Grove

In a grove where laughter rings,
Ancient trees dance with the wings.
Roots tangled in a jolly twist,
Whispers of the fruit they missed.

Squirrels squabble, tales they weave,
Of figs that had no time to cleave.
Each branch a legacy of cheer,
Echoes of fruit jokes through the year.

Nectar of the Past

Sweet nectar drips from cheeky fruit,
Sticky fingers, and clumsy boot.
Falling laughter from the trees,
Making mischief on the breeze.

Once upon a sunny day,
Figs conspired and laughed away.
They tossed their seeds with playful glee,
A legacy of comedy!

Tapestry of Treetops

A tapestry of leaves and laughs,
Figgy stories of joyous gaffes.
High above where giggles grew,
   Treetops whisper silly too.

Each branch a stage for nature's play,
   Fruity antics day by day.
   In the treetops tales unfold,
With colors bright and laughter bold.

Nectar of the Past

Once a fig fell from the tree,
Bounced and laughed, oh so free.
It rolled away, what a sight,
Charmed the ants with delight.

A grape joined in, made a scene,
Said, "You should've been a bean!"
But the fig just sweetly grinned,
And said, "I'm where the fun begins!"

Mosaic of Memories

In a jam jar, what a place,
Fig often dreams of a race.
With strawberries up ahead,
They chuckle, 'who'll end up spread?'

Peachy laughs, 'You're so last year!'
But fig just winks, full of cheer.
"Try to catch me if you can!"
And runs away just like a fan.

Roots That Bind

Underneath the ground they dive,
Roots are where the secrets thrive.
Fig whispers tales, oh so bright,
Of birds and bees that take flight.

"Remember when I turned to pie?"
"Or was it cake?" they all sigh.
Then the laughs start rolling in,
No dessert can quite top this win!

In the Shadow of Giants

Under trees that touch the sky,
Fig jokes, "What a way to fly!"
With acorns planning their big plays,
They scheme for sap and sunlit days.

But fig just chuckles, smiles wide,
"I'll take the breeze with style and pride."
In the shadow, it sings along,
As giants dance to its sweet song.

Vines and Verses

In a garden lush and grand,
Chill winds play a merry band.
With blushing cheeks, they shake and sway,
Bouncing fruits in bright array.

A chatter of leaves, what a delight,
Dance around with all their might.
Under the sun, they twist and curl,
Nature's jesters in a twirl.

Each vine has tales of laughter bright,
For who knew they could take flight?
With roots that giggle, branches tease,
Whispers float in the gentle breeze.

So gather round for tales anew,
Of juicy pranks and sticky goo.
In this realm where flavors gleam,
Life's a punchline—a fruity dream.

Chronicles of Soft Skins

Oh what tales the skins can tell,
Of sun-kissed days, they weave so well.
With squishy laughter, they invite,
To munch and crunch with pure delight.

From tiny seeds to great big fruits,
In stretchy shirts, they play their roots.
Each juicy nibble, a story spun,
A ticklish giggle, oh what fun!

The saga of the sap, so sweet,
Playing tricks on hungry feet.
One tiny bite, and boom—oh my!
A burst of sunshine and a pie in the sky!

So next time you see a fruit parade,
Remember the smiles that they have made.
For every skin is a passion play,
Tickling taste buds, come what may.

Beneath the Foliage

Under leaves, where shadows dance,
Funny critters take a chance.
With sly grins, they leap and glide,
Beneath the green, without a guide.

Mischief lurks in every nook,
Flavors fresh like a favorite book.
Juicy treasures are up for grabs,
While they giggle in leafy labs.

A tumble here, a roll there too,
Squirrels chuckle, and so do you.
Guardians of sweetness in this land,
Together they make a comical band.

So next time you wander through the green,
Listen for laughter—the best you've seen.
For beneath the foliage's playful guise,
There's a world of joy, a feast for the eyes.

Seeds of Serendipity

Scattered seeds in a jolly spree,
Sprout up giggles along with glee.
Each tiny orb a prankster bold,
Waiting for sunshine to unfold.

They tumble down with a playful hop,
Chasing dreams, they never stop.
With roots that whisper, tales of cheer,
Every sprout is a jester here.

In the garden of happenstance bright,
They play hide and seek with delight.
Each little wheat a laugh so grand,
A fertile breeze, a merry band.

So plant those seeds, let laughter grow,
In every corner, let joy overflow.
For serendipity's sing song calls,
To sprout a giggle where laughter falls.

Stories Woven in Flesh

In a garden, quite absurd,
Fruits whisper tales unheard.
With every bite, a giggle's shared,
Nature's jokes, oh how they dared.

Beneath the leaves, secrets sprawl,
A fruit's wisdom, who would call?
Skin so wrinkled, tales untold,
Laughter ripens, brave and bold.

Every tree a merry sage,
Fruits gathering, wisdom's wage.
They plan to throw a juicy feast,
With puns so ripe, the laugh's a beast.

So munch away, embrace the jest,
Each bite's a riddle, a fruit test.
In these stories, life connects,
With humor, nature plays and reflects.

Resonance of Ages

Old trees whisper, chuckle low,
Tales of yore, a comic show.
Their bounty, rich and sweetly wise,
Ancient pranks in nature's guise.

Each fruit a joke, quite well-rehearsed,
In sugary plots, the laughter burst.
Ripened secrets bounce around,
Echoes of humor, softly found.

Juicy legends, sticky and bright,
A fruit's mischief in the daylight.
Their vibrant squabbles, time's embrace,
Laughter rippling through the space.

Past and present twist and twine,
Crafting stories, oh so fine.
From orchard's heart, joy will spring,
Listen close, what laughter brings.

Soft Shadows and Sweetness

In the shade, where laughter grows,
Sweetest secrets, nature knows.
A fruit with mischief, full of mirth,
Whispers of humor circle the earth.

Giggles tumble down the vines,
With every grin, the sun aligns.
Beneath soft leaves, stories play,
A dance of joy, come what may.

Each tender bite, a jester's call,
Reminding us to laugh through it all.
With every crunch, a chuckle shared,
Fruitful mischief, ever bared.

So sip the nectar, sweet and bright,
Embrace the folly, pure delight.
In shadows soft, and sweetness true,
Laughter blooms from me and you.

A Fruitful Heritage

From branches thick, a legacy,
Of fruity humor, wild and free.
Plump with wisdom, sweet with jest,
Nature's punchlines, never rest.

Old branches sway, chuckling loud,
Underneath the leafy shroud.
With every harvest, tales arise,
Jokes buried deep in nature's guise.

A family tree of funny fruit,
Mirth and sweetness, absolute.
Roots entwined, a comedy,
Connected through this fruit-filled spree.

Come join the feast, take your slice,
In every bite, a little spice.
This heritage, so rich and grand,
Together we laugh, hand in hand.

Verdant Echoes

In the garden, green and bright,
A squirrel danced with pure delight.
He saw a fig, oh what a find,
I hope he's careful, he's so blind!

With every leap, he looked so spry,
But almost bumped into a pie.
Squeaky friends all gathered 'round,
For that fig, best snack found in town!

Sweetness Entwined

There's a fruit that's quite the tease,
It makes some giggle, others wheeze.
With skins so smooth and colors bright,
Some say they glow in the moonlight!

I took a bite, it burst with zest,
But left my dreams a sticky mess.
Now I'm a fig fan, can't you see?
Wishing for jam on toast for tea!

Echoes of the Bough

Underneath the fig tree's sway,
A group of ants had come to play.
One shouted, "Hey! Look what I found!"
A fig as big as they could hoound!

Their plan to snack turned quite absurd,
As a bird swooped down, quick as a blur.
The ants all laughed, and off they ran,
Squeaking out, "Guess we're not the plan!"

Tales from the Foliage

In a tree with leaves so fine,
There's a fig who thinks he's divine.
He flaunts his sweetness, puffs with pride,
But who would guess what's deep inside?

One day a ladybug took a peek,
And shouted out, "You're quite the freak!"
With seeds galore, he made a fuss,
"Not me! I'm just a fruit, not us!"

Harvested Dreams

In the garden, dreams do sprout,
With sneaky roots, they dance about.
They giggle when the sun goes down,
And whisper secrets to the clown.

Beneath the leaves, a treasure lies,
A tiny fruit in a big disguise.
It claims to be a great delight,
But rolls away and takes to flight!

The Jewel of the Garden

Nestled snug beneath the vine,
A gem that winks, 'Come taste, I shine!'
A critter hops, and then retreats,
For fancy fruit beats tiny treats.

With ruffled leaves and leafy flair,
It giggles loud without a care.
'Pick me first!' it starts to shout,
While other fruits just pout and doubt.

Seasons of Harvest

Spring brings hope with colors bright,
While summer's warmth ignites delight.
But just when you think it's your year,
Out pops a squirrel with a sneaky cheer!

Autumn vibes start to appear,
With harvest joy and autumn beer.
Yet who knew, oh what a plight,
That veggies laugh and have a bite!

The Gifts of Time

In the garden, time does play,
With ripe surprises planned each day
You blink your eyes, it seems to tease,
And suddenly, there's fruit with ease!

Each ripe round shape tells a tale,
Of silly gnomes and windy gales.
So whenever you feel in a funk,
Just check the patch for a funny plum!

Whispers of Sweet Succulence

In a market bustling with delight,
Fruits of purple tease the sight.
They whisper secrets, oh so sweet,
Of sticky fingers and juicy treats.

A squirrel tried to take a bite,
But dropped it, what a comical sight!
Rolling away as if in despair,
The fruit just giggled in the air.

Cooks with recipes grand and bold,
Dream of jam that never grows old.
They dance with jars that gleam and shine,
While sticky fingers sneak at lunchtime.

A fruit that's famous for being round,
Once tried to pick a fight with a hound.
But laughter burst from the pup's big grin,
As the sweet fruit just rolled on in.

Beneath the Ancient Tree

Beneath the tree that knows no age,
Fruits debate the latest rage.
A berry claims to be the best,
While other fruits just laugh and jest.

"I'm sweeter than your sappy line!"
Said one with bravado, all divine.
But the apple chimed in, "Oh please,
I'm what the teachers call a tease!"

The pear just rolled its greenish eye,
"I'm the one that gets the pie!"
And so they argue day and night,
Beneath the tree, what a silly sight!

Then comes the wind, with a gusty laugh,
Sending all their chatter down the path.
They tumble and twirl, a fruity mess,
And giggle at nature's grand silliness.

Fruits of Forgotten Time

Once there was a fruit with tales,
Of pirates, ships, and blooming gales.
It claimed its juice could grant a wish,
But all could do was make a squish.

A traveler heard the fruit's grand lore,
To find it, he climbed a mountain sore.
But upon his reach, with a mighty cheer,
He found it squashed, "Oh, dear!"

With laughter loud, the fruit replied,
"Your wishes are better served outside!"
And so it rolled away with flair,
To spread the joy that filled the air.

Now legends whisper of its fame,
Of sticky shoes and fruity game.
All who seek it must remember this,
The journey's fun is the sweetest bliss!

Legacy of the Silken Skin

There once was fruit with silky skin,
Adventurers sought it with a grin.
But each time they reached, it slipped away,
And left them laughing at their play.

"Oh, I'm just practicing for the ball!"
The fruit would tease, all dressed in thrall.
With a twirl and a twist, it'd always evade,
While the explorers' dreams began to fade.

Then came a child, with pure delight,
Whistling a tune, oh what a sight!
The fruit, enchanted, stopped in its track,
And giggled, "Well, you've got the knack!"

Together they danced under the moon,
Beneath stars that hummed a silly tune.
And the fruit learned joy from the child's wide grin,
A legacy of laughter that draws us in.

Ciphers in the Leaves

Whispers seeping through the trees,
Deciphering jokes in the gentle breeze.
Each leaf a riddle, green and bright,
Tickling fancies in morning light.

Squirrels giggle as they climb,
Plotting mischief, oh so sublime.
Acorn knighthood in a playful fight,
Guarding treasures 'til the night.

A woodpecker's tap, a drummer's beat,
Nature's band playing tunes so sweet.
Every rustle gives a hint,
Of hidden tales that leave us in sprint.

Tickled by shadows, dancing about,
The trees sway, we laugh and shout.
Ciphers call out, an impertinent tease,
In this circus, I find my ease.

Harvesting Hope

In the orchard where laughter blooms,
Hope swings high, dispelling glooms.
Gathering dreams in baskets wide,
Every fruit a giggle, a playful ride.

Pickin' pears in the sunny haze,
Bumbling bees in a buzzing daze.
A peach slips, causing a scene,
Who knew farming could be so keen?

Ripe tomatoes in a tumble-down,
Rolling 'round on the farmyard ground.
The chickens laugh, their feathers fluffed,
Clucking secrets, never enough!

Plucking hope from vine and tree,
It's a silly fest, come dance with me.
Harvesting joy, the sweetest chore,
In this patch, who could ask for more?

Stories in the Sap

Sticky tales drip from the bark,
With every drop, we light a spark.
Whimsical stories in amber hues,
When listening close, you hear the blues.

A spider spins lace, a poet's dream,
Too busy weaving to hear the scream.
The sap runs thick with giggles and grins,
A comedy club for all of us kin.

Ants march by, their tiny parade,
Swapping stories, shade in the glade.
The trees chuckle, swaying around,
Revealing the laughter that's always found.

With every rise and the sudden fall,
Sticky sap keeps sharing its all.
Join the tales, a bustling crowd,
In these woods, let joy be loud!

Beneath the Weeping Canopy

Underneath the leafy veil,
Lies a world of whimsy and nonchalant tale.
Teardrops glisten, but don't you fret,
It's just the branches getting wet.

Giggling flowers, waving hello,
Every petal dancing, putting on a show.
A rabbit hops by, sings a tune,
Melodies matching the afternoon.

Shadows play tricks on wandering feet,
Is that a ghost, or just my seat?
The breeze joins in, a playful tease,
Movement so silly, it's sure to please.

Whimsical whispers in a green embrace,
Where every drop holds a funny face.
Beneath this canopy, laughter springs,
In this melody of life, my heart sings!

Fruits of Yesterday

Once a fruit so round and sweet, Telling tales of summer heat. It droops and laughs, it leaks a bit, Best not to wear a sticky fit.

Worms throw parties all night long, Singing silly tunes and songs. A squirrel darts, with cheeky flair, Claiming harvest—it's only fair!

A wiggle here, a wobble there, Who knew fruit could cause such scare? A juicy plume, it starts to roll, Keeping secrets—oh, what a hole!

In jars it hides from hungry eyes, Where even ants can't form a line. It dreams of pies and tasty treats, As it turns from sweets to beats.

Beneath the Gnarled Branches

Beneath the branches, shadows dance, Where fruits forget their weighty stance. They giggle as they tumble down, What a sight, oh what a clown!

The bees take bets on fruity spins, As squirrels plan their sneaky wins. With acorns stacked like cozy beds, Who'll grab the prize? It spills, it spreads!

A pear just stumbles, snags its friend, The antics never seem to end. They form a gang, with puns galore, Grapefruit grins, and cherries roar.

In this patch, the laughter flows, A fruity circus, who really knows? With juicy jokes and fruity pings, Who needs a crown when you have wings?

Whispers of Sweetness

In the garden, a chatter grows, Where sweetness hides in silly rows. Bananas boast and apples tease, Grapes raise glasses, "More, if you please!"

Beneath the sun, they weave their tales, Of flavors fierce and fruity gales. Orange jokes, and lemon puns, Creating mischief, laughter runs.

Strawberries share their bold confessions, About jam-making obsessions. While peaches roll with giggly glee, Simple fruits, such matchmakers be!

The whispers float on breezy trails, Of berry minds and tart details. In fruity gossip, there's no strife, Just laughable tales of fruit-filled life.

Beneath the Leafy Canopy

Beneath the leaves, the shadows play, A stroll through fruit, hip-hip-hooray! With berries bouncing, and melons proud, Each rusty laugh forms a fruity crowd.

The lemons wear their sunny hats, While mangoes tango with the cats. Figs try to jump, but miss the beat, Get yourself a fruity seat!

The lush green stage, they share their jokes, A grape once claimed it could lift folks. As laughter echoes, fruits collide, In sweet mayhem, what a ride!

Beneath this canopy so wide, The fruits laugh off the morning tide. A fruity circus, bright and fun, They toast to joy, 'til day is done!

Nature's Culinary Secrets

In gardens where the critters creep,
The fruits of laughter, secrets keep.
A plump delight hangs low and bright,
With bites of joy, a tasty bite.

A squirrel stole a piece to munch,
He danced a jig, oh what a lunch!
The whispers of the trees conspire,
To share a snack that does inspire.

With every taste, the giggles grow,
A festival of flavors flow.
In every dish, a tale is spun,
Of how this fruity prank was done.

So gather round, don't miss the fun,
Let nature's meal for everyone!
With playful bites and joyous cheer,
The food of life is always near.

The Aroma of Legacy

A waft of sweetness fills the air,
As critters dart without a care.
The scent of mischief, oh so bold,
In every bite, a tale unfolds.

A raccoon donned a chef's white hat,
And stirred up nuts, imagine that!
With giggles shared and spoons askew,
The feast was grand, but not for two.

As bees buzzed in, they joined the fray,
They dipped and danced in joyous play.
The banquet grew, oh what a thrill,
With flavors wild, they chomped their fill.

So raise a toast to culinary games,
The laughter rings, we share our names.
For in each bite, a tale we weave,
Of silly meals, we all believe.

The Comfort of Juicy Warmth

Upon a branch, a treasure swings,
So juicy sweet, it never stings.
With every taste, a smile in bloom,
A comfort found, dispelling gloom.

A bunny hopped to join the spree,
With sticky paws and glee, oh me!
The warmth of sun kissed every bite,
A joyful feast in pure delight.

The laughter echoed through the trees,
As neighbors feasted with such ease.
Each shared morsel, a silly thrust,
In nature's warmth, it's joy we trust.

So gather up, both near and far,
This juicy treat is quite bizarre!
With laughter shared 'neath leafy crown,
The comfort found, we'll never frown.

Cradled in Nature's Hands

In nature's arms, a banquet grows,
With funny tales that everyone knows.
A hidden gem beneath the leaves,
Where laughter dances, joy retrieves.

A parrot squawks with perfect flair,
As grapes rain down, a feathery scare!
With every plop, a chuckle bursts,
An orchestra of nature's thirsts.

A family of ducks waddled by,
In search of treats, oh me, oh my!
With wiggly worms and crumbs of bread,
Together they shared the overflow spread.

So here's to fun in every bite,
Cradled in hands, oh pure delight.
Beneath the sun, we play our part,
With nature's feast to warm the heart.

Echoes in Orchard Shadows

In the orchard where shadows dance,
The green figs plot their silly prance.
They quip and giggle, oh what a sight,
Making the sunniest day feel just right.

With every pluck, a story unfurls,
Of fruit fights and giddy swirls.
Pies in the making, laughter loud,
Even the trees are feeling proud.

A Harvest of Memories

Every bite brings a chuckle anew,
As memories pop like apples in stew.
Fallen fruit makes for slippery slips,
Laughing at those who dare take sips.

Grandma's pie, it made us cheer,
Spilling creamy bits and giggles near.
The dog in pursuit, with a gleeful yowl,
Chasing after crumbs like a culinary howl.

Seeds of Solitude

In solitude, I munch alone,
Figs in hand, like royalty on a throne.
They whisper secrets, juicy and sweet,
Contagious laughter with every treat.

But who needs friends with figs around?
They make absurd flavors quite profound.
A fig in each hand, a song in the air,
Harmony's humor—life's funny affair.

The Luscious Heritage

From ancient roots to modern glee,
Figs have thrived through history.
With a twist and a turn, on table so bare,
They bring delightful antics to share.

In jam or in cake, they're quite the show,
Their playful nature making friendships grow.
We raise a toast to this luscious crew,
For laughter's sweet essence is crafted anew.

Echoes of the Grove

In the grove where laughter swells,
Fruits hold court and tell their tales.
A pear once slipped, a berry swayed,
The antics bright, the sun's parade.

The rabbits danced, the squirrels pranced,
In leafy hats, they took their chance.
With tiny drinks, they made a toast,
To fruits that grow and cause a boast.

Amid the chaos, shadows skim,
An owl hoots loud, as lights grow dim.
The wind, it chuckles, rustles down,
As laughter echoes all around.

So here's to jests and fruit delight,
A grove alive with silly sights.
With every bite, indulge and grin,
For laughter's sweet—the best within.

A Festival of Flavors

A festival blooms, oh what a sight,
With jam-filled jars, a true delight.
The strawberries juggle, peaches sing,
It's a fruity show, come join the fling!

A pineapple winks, a melon bows,
As nutty friends perform their vows.
Together they prance, a merry crew,
While the lemon drops dance—who knew?

With tastes that burst, the laughter flows,
As plummy pies steal the show, who knows!
A sour face? Just squeeze it tight,
And taste the joy, it's pure delight!

So come one, come all, let's share a cheer,
In fruity land, there's nothing to fear.
With giggles sweet as candied bliss,
This festival's one you won't want to miss!

Leaves of Abundance

Beneath the leaves, a party brews,
Where legume hats and fruit prunes choose.
The cucumbers giggle, peeking through,
With broccoli hats, made just for two.

A cabbage rolls, and what a mess,
As tomatoes claim the title, 'Best Dress!'
In this leafy realm, they prance and whirl,
The gardens bloom—oh what a swirl!

An eggplant juggles, trying too hard,
While peppers squabble—oh so marred!
With every crunch, the fun expands,
Together they make the silliest bands.

So when you wander through this bliss,
Or munch a leaf, don't forget to kiss
The joy from roots and leaves so stout,
In nature's dance, there's never doubt!

Rooted in Tradition

An old tree sways with stories told,
Of roots and shoots, and fruits of gold.
With each new spring, the laughter grows,
As merry boughs wear nature's clothes.

The wise old trunk leans back with glee,
Recalling whispers from the bee.
The branches nod in playful jest,
While dance of shadows takes the quest.

A nutty tale, a barky joke,
With all around, a merry cloak.
Traditions bloom, a vibrant cheer,
As nature's laughter fills the sphere.

So raise a glass of sap, my friend,
To roots so deep that never end.
For in this grove, the jig is real,
A kaleidoscope of fun we feel!

Nectar's Embrace

In a grove where fruits collide,
Figs giggle, with pride they abide.
Sticky fingers in a race,
Joyful laughter fills the space.

Birds wear hats made of green leaves,
Chasing shadows, they tease and weave.
A squirrel dances, quite a sight,
In the sun, everything's bright.

Bumblebees buzz with a plan,
Teaching flowers how to jam.
Nature's rhythm, sweet and bold,
Every story, new and old.

At dusk, the stars begin to wink,
Figs sharing secrets in a blink.
Laughter bounces, echoing true,
In this grove where fun breaks through.

Tales from the Fig Grove

Under branches wide and strong,
Figs gather 'round for a song.
With wit and charm, they converse,
In every tale, there's averse.

A wise old owl shares a jest,
While a baby fig laughs the best.
Gopher jokes, and crows reply,
Creating chaos in the sky.

The wind plays tricks, turning leaves,
The figs giggle, as one believes.
With every poke of nature's hand,
New tales arise, spontaneous and grand.

As moonlight dances on the floor,
Figs trade stories, seeking more.
Each laugh a seed, a sprout of glee,
In their grove, forever free.

Threads of Time

Figs weave stories, strands so fine,
Each year adds a twist to the line.
With every season changing hue,
Laughter sprouts, as if brand new.

Old fig trees whisper secrets low,
Sharing tales of long ago.
A mischievous breeze tugs at their bark,
Sparking giggles, lighting a spark.

A rabbit quips, 'Time's just a jest,'
As birds chirp songs, they never rest.
Each moment's caught in nature's fold,
Funny mishaps, forever told.

And as the sun sets, colors blend,
The figs conclude, 'This is the end.'
Yet, tomorrow brings stories anew,
In the threads of time, lives review.

The Fruit Still Remains

In the orchard ripe with cheer,
Figs boast of their fruity sphere.
Competition's fierce, but all in fun,
Who'll be topped? Just wait, till done.

Caterpillars munch on dreams,
While ants host wild, buzzing schemes.
Each piece of fruit a claim to fame,
As insects join in on the game.

Silly stains of sweetness cling,
To every creature, they begin to sing.
The fruitcake's now a fig delight,
With giggles during every bite.

And though time may pass, they hold fast,
The memories, like shadows cast.
With laughter still echoing clear,
The sweetness and joy—they endear.

Beneath Starlit Boughs

Beneath the trees where shadows play,
The critters dance till break of day.
A squirrel claims his prize with flair,
While raccoons waltz without a care.

Branches draped in moonlight's grace,
A party held in nature's space.
The figs, they giggle, ripe and round,
As laughter echoes all around.

But when a bird sings out a tune,
The raccoons hide—oh, what a swoon!
For all their bravado, they are shy,
Underneath the twinkling sky.

Yet every night when stars appear,
A secret world draws close and near.
Old roots and tales, they intertwine,
In simple joy, our hearts align.

Fruits of Forgotten Stories

Where stories linger, ripe and sweet,
A fig tree grows, oh what a treat!
Beneath its branches, tales unfold,
Of daring deeds and dreams of old.

A fox once tried to steal a bite,
But ended up in quite a plight!
With sticky paws and giggles loud,
He pranced around, a jester proud.

The wind whispers secrets in the air,
Of goofy gnomes who dance with flair.
Each fruit a witness, each leaf a page,
To laughter shared throughout the age.

So gather 'round, both young and bold,
For fruits of laughter never get old.
And as the night begins to fall,
Sip sweet memories, one and all.

The Tree of Abundance

In a garden where the laughter grows,
A tree stands tall, where fun bestows.
Its branches heavy, fruit adorned,
Beneath its shade, joy is born.

A hungry hare with grand designs,
Proclaims, "These figs should all be mine!"
But squirrels tease him, darting quick,
While wise old tortoises just stick.

A feast erupts, with snacks galore,
And critters gather, wanting more.
The figs all giggle in delight,
As chaos reigns 'neath warm moonlight.

With every bite and every cheer,
They celebrate the bonds so dear.
For in abundance, we all agree,
A world of fun, is best; you see!

Shades of Resilience

In the shadow of a mighty tree,
The figs conspire, oh what a spree!
They whisper tales of inane schemes,
And laughter weaves through shadowed dreams.

The parrot squawks, with flair so grand,
"These fruits are best! Come take my hand!"
But even as the mischief swells,
The stories bloom where laughter dwells.

Although the storms may rage and roar,
The tree stands firm, a trusted shore.
Under its leaves, life's quirks unite,
As critters share their silly plight.

So raise a toast to roots so deep,
To silly dreams and all we keep.
In every fig, a spark of cheer,
A legacy of joy appears.

Pathways of the Past

In a garden of wonder, a journey begins,
With branches like sneakers, and some silly grins.
They laugh at the squirrels, those cheeky little jesters,
Plotting grand heists like miniature testers.

Through pathways of green, with secrets untold,
The roots whisper stories, both daring and bold.
Little critters dance on the leaves of nostalgia,
While pigeons on patrol form their own band of euphoria.

With each step they take, a giggle is shared,
As petals drop softly, no one seems scared.
The echoes of laughter are what truly last,
In the maze of this garden, they're having a blast.

So if ever you wander this whimsical lane,
Remember the joy that it gladly retains.
For under the sun, in this leafy cast,
You'll find fun and magic – it's far from the past!

A Story in Every Bite

Take a nibble of sweetness, a taste so divine,
With each little slice, it's an adventure in line.
From the tree's funny face, to the one in the pie,
Each morsel a story, oh me, oh my!

There's gossip in flavor, a banquet of tales,
Each bite is a journey as laughter prevails.
With honeyed delights that dance on your tongue,
It's like a wild party where everyone's young.

The cake in the oven, a fragrant delight,
Shouts to the world, "Come savor the night!"
There's fig in the punch, and the punchline is clear,
Just one little sip and you'll burst out in cheer!

So gather your friends, for a feast you can't smite,
For there's laughter and flavor, a marvelous sight.
With each delicious bite, let joy be our guide,
For life is a banquet where happiness won't hide.

The Majestic Blossom

In a garden of giggles, a bloom takes its stand,
With petals like confetti, it's humor unplanned.
The bees throw a party, their dance is a spree,
As they buzz 'round the blossoms, oh what glee!

The spindly stems sway like they're in a ball,
With a twist and a turn, they dance through it all.
Each petal is painted with colors so bright,
It's a comedic sketch in the evening light.

The sun's golden laughter spills over the scene,
As flowers exchange jokes; it's a vibrant routine.
With a wink and a nod, they sway to the tune,
Of breezes that giggle beneath the full moon.

So when you see blooms, take a moment to stop,
Join the party of petals that never will drop.
For in every blossom, a funny little quirk,
Is the laughter of nature, a playful perk.

Silent Witness to Time

Beneath ancient branches where stories unfold,
The tree chuckles softly, its wisdom is bold.
It's seen every dance, every leap and each fall,
A witness to laughter, it's heard it all.

When seasons come calling, it waves them hello,
With whispers of chaos, oh how breezes blow!
While squirrels hold conferences, quite serious affairs,
The tree simply laughs at their well-dressed airs.

With rings like a diary, each year carved in place,
It chuckles at time and its slow, strange pace.
For in every wrinkle, a joke can be found,
In the laughter of ages, joy's ever around.

So, gather your friends and rest by its side,
Share stories with the tree, let the humor abide.
For in its old branches, the fun never ends,
As it cradles our laughter and all that descends.

Circles of Life

In a garden where mischief grows,
A fig tree dances with jolly toes.
The squirrels plot their acorn heist,
While the birds chirp tales of feathery zest.

Down comes a cat with a wobbly stride,
Thinking it's a great place to hide.
But right on cue, a fig drops low,
And the surprise makes the kitty go 'whoa!'

The jester rabbit hops in delight,
Hoping the figs will give him a bite.
He winks at the crow, who's eyeing the snack,
But the figs just rolled away—what a whack!

At the end of the day, with giggles and cheer,
The garden bursts into a vibrant sphere.
Life spins in circles, laughter ignites,
In the orchard of joy, where mischief's in sights!

Tales of a Tender Branch

A tender branch sways soft and sweet,
Whispers to lovers, a love so fleet.
"Come pluck my fruit!" it sings with glee,
But watch for the bees—they're stingers, you see!

A wise old owl perches up high,
He tells the tales with a twinkle in eye.
"Those figs hold secrets—juicy, divine,
Just mind your manners, and you'll be just fine."

The ants in a row march under the sun,
Planning a feast—oh, it's sure to be fun!
But one little ant trips on a fig,
Now we've got tumble bugs doing a jig!

Under the moonlight, the laughter grows loud,
As shadows play games, a whimsical crowd.
The night blooms with stories, both wacky and grand,
Beneath that tender branch, we all take a stand!

Beneath the Summer Sun

Beneath the sun, the figs do glow,
A shimmering treat, a radiant show.
But beware the seagull, with a mischievous eye,
He swoops down low, oh me, oh my!

The children giggle, running on grass,
As a fig rolls by, they all let it pass.
"Let's compete!" says one with a pout,
"To see who can catch it—doubt there's a route!"

A playful breeze sneaks through the leaves,
Whispering tales that a heart believes.
It tickles the toes of those who dare,
To taste a slice of this summer air!

As laughter echoes, nature joins in,
With the clinks of glee, let the fun begin.
In the warmth of the sun, all worries can flit,
For beneath that bright sky, it's just charm, and wit!

Fruition of Dreams

In the land of dreams, where figs take flight,
A jester in fruit form dances at night.
The moon giggles softly, casting its gleam,
As all come together in a figgy dream.

An elephant trumpets with joy and grace,
"Let's have a party in this figgy place!"
The hippos join in, with a bashful sway,
While the figs laugh along, "We're the stars of the day!"

Beneath twinkling lights, the fun starts to brew,
With dances and prances, a most splendid view.
"More figs!" shout the folks—what a sight to behold,
As giggles erupt from the hints of the bold.

With each little bite, the laughter does swell,
In this realm of fruit, all is jolly and swell.
So here's to the dreams that frolic and scheme,
In a world full of laughter, it's the fig's finest theme!

Echoes of Eden

In gardens lush where laughter thrived,
The fruits of joy were much contrived.
A waddle here, a wiggle there,
The squirrels plotted without a care.

Old Adam snickered, Eve just rolled,
They sold their fig for coins of gold.
Yet in the shade, they'd often gloat,
For every fruit was worth a quote.

A parrot squawking wise old tales,
Of figgy feasts and jolly gales.
It seems that laughter's seeds were sown,
In every bite, a giggle grown.

So if you find a garden rife,
With quirky trees and juicy life,
Just know the humor lingers still,
In every fig, a jovial thrill.

Under the Fig's Canopy

Underneath this wobbly tree,
I spotted quite absurdity.
A family of ants in a conga line,
Dancing like they've had too much wine.

The figs above just swung and swayed,
While nature's comedy played displayed.
Each plump fruit dangled, full of dreams,
But ants just served them with ice cream schemes.

A curious cat with a wobbly strut,
Thought for a moment that she was cut.
But a fig fell down, and with a leap,
She found herself in a giggle deep.

So gather here for fruity fun,
Under this canopy, one by one.
The laughter echoes, round and round,
In every fig, pure joy is found.

The Color of Memory

Memory's color, a vibrant hue,
Painted in figs and laughter too.
Old stories wrapped in sweet delight,
Fill up the day and lighten the night.

The painter dips her brush so wide,
Each stroke is playful, nothing to hide.
With giggles mixed in every shade,
Life's canvas bright, with joy, it's laid.

A watercolor of friends and fun,
With syrupy laughter that can't outrun.
Figs spill stories in each bite,
Transforming gloom into sheer delight.

So let your memories burst like fruit,
With joyous colors, never mute.
In every hue, a chuckle rolls,
Life's the fig that fills our souls.

Ancient Roots, New Blooms

Ancient roots which tickle the ground,
In figgy laughter, wisdom's found.
The tales they tell, all twisted and funny,
Of dancing blooms and drops of honey.

Old boasts of figs so grand and bold,
Mix with whispers of secrets told.
The branches sway, each laugh a cheer,
Inviting all to gather near.

The blooms arise with comic flair,
Waving jokes on the summer air.
A bee buzzes in to join the jest,
Creating buzz that never rests.

So laugh along with nature's rhyme,
In every fig, you'll find your time.
With roots so rich and blooms so rare,
The jest of life is everywhere.

The Color of Memory

In sepia tones and soft pastels,
The figs remember their grand hotels.
With each sweet nibble, a tale unfolds,
Of frolicsome feasts and laughter retold.

Bright colors dance in every bite,
They glimmer like stars in the night.
A fig once wore a royal crown,
Until ants showed up and burned it down.

Among the branches, stories intertwine,
About lost socks and silly wine.
The fruit whispers to those who dare,
"Join in the jest, it's only fair!"

With smiles and giggles through and through,
The memories, hilarious and true.
In every fig that comes to feast,\nAre laughs and colors, to say the least.

Seasons of the Soul

In springtime, fruits like jokes arise,
A dance with branches 'neath sunny skies.
We laugh at blossoms, quite absurd,
Petals tumbling, wisdom unheard.

In summer's heat, we sip some tea,
While squirrels debate philosophy.
They chatter on about the best
Nuts for hosting their grand fest.

Autumn leaves, they waltz so bold,
Telling tales of days of old.
Each crunch beneath our clumsy feet,
A light-hearted autumnal beat.

In winter's chill, we cozy up tight,
Sharing stories by firelight.
We giggle at frost-covered trees,
Whispering secrets to the breeze.

Sweetness of the Past

Once there was a fruit so sweet,
Naughty kids snuck bites to eat.
They'd giggle 'fore their mother came,
Hiding evidence, playing the game.

Beneath the tree, they would conspire,
Dreaming big, with hearts on fire.
Each sticky finger, a secret tried,
In that orchard, they would bide.

As years roll on, they're grown and wise,
Still chuckling at those fruity lies.
For sweetness lingers, a playful ghost,
In memories, they cherish the most.

And every now and then, on a dare,
They'll visit that tree and breathe the air.
Remembering roots and childhood games,
Those sweetened days with silly names.

Whispers of Kindred Spirits

Gathered 'round in twilight's glow,
Whispers float where laughter flows
Fruits of wisdom and nutty tales,
Of flying dreams and epic fails.

Old friends bumping with glee so bright,
Sharing snacks and silly bites.
They muse on life's wacky turns,
Each chuckle shared, the spirit burns.

"Do figs really dance when no one sees?"
A question floats carried by the breeze.
"Of course they do," a voice pops in,
"Especially when the moon wears a grin!"

They toast to quirks both near and far,
Under stars that shine like a bizarre bazaar.
For in each laugh, a bond is spun,
Kindred spirits, forever young.

Lush Layers of History

In layers thick, our past resides,
With comical twists and foolish prides.
Old relics smile and sometimes smirk,
Sharing secrets of their quirky work.

History's fables, so tasty and bright,
Serve up laughter in the night.
Each ancient tale, a delightful cheat,
Crunchy and crispy, oh, what a treat!

A time machine made of ripe delights,
Takes us on misadventures and flights.
Tomfoolery bound in every vine,
We nibble on past, it tastes divine.

So gather 'round for the fruit of lore,
With giggles and snickers, we all explore.
For in each layer, we find a way,
To celebrate history, and laugh all day.

The Clock of Seasons

The clock ticks joyfully, with fruits galore,
Each hour a snack, who could ask for more?
Peaches go plump, and apples wear crowns,
While lemons just smile, never wearing frowns.

The spring brings a dance, all flowers in line,
Bees buzzing freely, sipping on wine.
But summer's a trickster, with heat on the rise,
Melons get bashful, hiding their size.

Autumn's the joker, with colors so bright,
Pumpkins wear costumes, a comical sight.
As winter rolls in, it whispers and hums,
Then Santa gets lost in the piles of plums.

So here's to the seasons, each wacky delight,
A clock made of laughter, from morning to night.

Autumn's Embrace

Autumn's a chubby, jolly old friend,
Pulling out sweaters, as summer must end.
Leaves do the cha-cha, rustling with glee,
While chestnuts get roasted, auditioning free.

Squirrels stockpile, with acorns galore,
Hiding their treasures, oh what a chore!
Pumpkins in patches, dressed up for a show,
Scarecrows just laugh, as the wind starts to blow.

Hot cider is bubbling, with flavors so bold,
But watch out for bees, who still want the gold.
Autumn's a riot, like a party unplanned,
With costumes and mischief, it's all close at hand.

So hold on to laughter, in this playful season,
Autumn's embrace is the best kind of reason.

Legacy of the Green

In gardens of giggles, the veggies all play,
Carrots wear hats, in a colorful way.
Tomatoes are blushing, quite red in their pride,
While cucumbers mimic, with their smooth little slide.

Onions have layers, but joke with no tears,
They tell silly tales, and keep out the fears.
Beans climb the fence, all tangled in cheer,
While potatoes chuckle, in the warmth of the sphere.

Herbs speak in whispers, oh fragrant and bright,
Basil's a poet, with words of delight.
Chives are the jesters, with quips sharp and neat,
Gardens are legends, where laughter's a treat.

So join in the fun, as the green takes its stand,
A legacy blooming, in this laughter-filled land.

Gardener's Remembrance

A gardener sneezes, oh pollen galore,
Amongst all the daisies, just outside the door.
She talks to her tulips, who giggle and sway,
While zucchinis gossip about yesterday.

With pots all around, like a circus in bloom,
Each plant has a story, and plenty of room.
The spiders are scholars, weaving their tales,
While rainbows of petals put boredom to scales.

Weeds throw a party, they're lively and spry,
But the gardener shows them just how to comply.
Roses get flustered with thorns as their style,
But they smile with grace, and that's worth the while.

So here's to the memories, both wild and serene,
In gardens of laughter, where joy's evergreen.

Celestial Delicacies

In a garden where oddities grow,
Little fruits wear a shimmering glow.
They giggle and dance in the breezy air,
Inviting all critters to join their affair.

With a sly wink, they whisper their names,
'Plump and juicy, we're wild little games!'
Even the bees buzz in silly delight,
As they feast on the sweets past the starry night.

One fruit in a hat claimed to be wise,
'Life's all about laughter and pies!'
But when others tried, they just got a smudge,
Leaving behind a giggling grudge.

So gather your friends for the jolly spree,
In the orchard of jests, we're all young and free!
With every bite, there's a smirk or a chat,
For no fruit is sweeter than the joyful act!

Midnight Harvest

Under the moon, a quirky crew gathers,
With baskets in hand, they share hearty blathers.
They sneak through the garden, quite the sight,
Picking fruits that sparkle under the night.

They trip over roots, with a splash and a shout,
Finding treasures that make them pout.
A rogue berry rolls and a toe it did stub,
'This harvest be brutal, just look at the hubbub!'

But oh, the sweetness, oh what a tease,
They chuckle and giggle with every squeeze.
A mishap here or an oops over there,
Turns their harvest into a joke-filled affair.

So raise a toast to the midnight spree,
With clumsy delight, they dance wild and free.
Each fruit is a story, each laugh a delight,
As they feast on their spoils till the morning light!

Tasting Time

Gather round, it's that time of year,
For fruits of delight and laughter we cheer.
With snacks on the table and smiles so bright,
We shop for our flavors, what a silly sight!

One plump berry boasts of its sweet, juicy fame,
While a skittish grape tries to join in the game.
With bravado, they bite into citrus galore,
And end up covered in juice on the floor.

Coffee and figs had a dance on the trunk,
They spun in a circle and gave quite a funk.
A lemon then hollered, 'I'm zestfully grand!'
'They're all juicing around because I'm in command!'

So let laughter erupt with every sweet taste,
In our funny little world, there's no time to waste.
We'll munch and we'll crunch till the sun goes down,
With fruit juice mustaches and laughter all around!

Threads of Nostalgia

In an attic of memories, we unearth a tale,
Of fruit-filled adventures that never go stale.
A jar of jam whispers secrets it keeps,
Of summers long gone and giggles in heaps.

Tangled in laughter, the stories unfold,
With sticky hands and mischief untold.
Grandma's sweet pies were a family affair,
But she always denied her secret recipe flair.

Now we squabble for slices with playful disdain,
'Who stole the last piece?!' starts up the refrain.
With crumbs in our beards, we can't help but grin,
For every sweet memory invites us back in.

As dusk falls softly, we raise our mugs high,
To fruity adventures beneath the big sky.
In threads of sweet laughter that tie us as one,
Our hearts and our tastes have nowhere to run!

Echoing Youthful Summers

In gardens bright, where shadows play,
We'd munch on fruit, not care for day.
With sticky hands and giggles loud,
We'd dance around, a silly crowd.

The sun would shine, the bugs would hum,
Our laughter mixed with a distant drum.
A tree we'd climb, up to the sky,
With dreams as big as the birds that fly.

Each bite we took, a burst of cheer,
While squirrels plotted mischief near.
We'd wager on who'd steal the last,
And end the day, our roots amassed.

So here we sit, all grown and wise,
With joyful hearts, we reminisce the prize.
Though life moves on, the joy won't fade,
For every summer, sweet memories made.

The Language of Leaves

Leaves whisper secrets, stories untold,
While squirrels argue, oh so bold.
They talk of figs and summer rain,
In the shade, we can't complain.

With laughter ringing, munching away,
The branches sway, the kids will play.
A game of hide-and-seek begins,
As bees buzz gently, lost in spins.

The elders smile, citing past fun,
'You won't believe how we used to run!'
While the young ones giggle, unsure of the tale,
Their faces sticky, with sweet detail.

In murmurs soft, the leaves agree,
Chasing joy is key, you see!
From roots to crown, let laughter grow,
For in this shade, we steal the show.

www.ingramcontent.com/pod-product-compliance
Lightning Source LLC
Chambersburg PA
CBHW060127230426
43661CB00003B/356